Mystical revelations receive the Imprimatur of The Church when they are judged to be in line with the Catholic doctrine and morals. An Imprimatur is Latin for "let it be printed". These revelations are meant to fill in the gaps left in the Bible because of censorship in the earlier days of the Christian Faith and also due to errors of translation. They reveal the things that happened as they happened. They are <u>not</u> meant to replace the Bible.

Books in this series

The Full of Grace: The Early Years.

The Full of Grace: The Merit.

The Full of Grace: Joseph's Passion.

The Full of Grace: The Blue Angel.

The Full of Grace: The Boyhood of Jesus.

The Chronicles of Jesus and the Apostles

Treasure with Seven Names-The Mark of the Apostles

The Chronicles of Jesus and Judas Iscariot

Jesus and Judas Iscariot-The Conversion

Lamb Books
Illustrated adaptations for the whole family

LAMB BOOKS

Published by Lamb Books, 2 Dalkeith Court, 45 Vincent Street, London SW1P 4HH;

UK, USA, FR, IT, SP, DE

www.lambbooks.org

First published by Lamb Books 2013
This edition
001

Text copyright @ Lamb Books Nominee, 2013

Illustrations copyright @ Lamb Books, 2013
The moral right of the author and illustrator has been asserted
All rights reserved

The author and publisher are grateful to the Centro Editoriale Valtoriano in Italy for Permission to quote from the Poem of the Man- God by Maria Valtorta, by Valtorta Publishing

Set in Bookman Old style
Printed and bound by CPI Group (UK) Ltd, Croydon, CR0, 4YY

Except in the USA, this book is sold subject to the condition that it shall not, by way of trade or otherwise, be lent, resold, hired out, or otherwise circulated without the publisher's prior consent in any form of binding or cover other than that in which it is published and without a similar condition including this condition being imposed on the subsequent purchaser

ISBN: 978-1-910201-04-6

The Full of Grace

The Boyhood of Jesus

LAMBBOOKS

Acknowledgements

The material in this book is adapted from The Mystical City of God, by Sister Mary of Jesus of Agreda, which received the Imprimatur in 1949 and also from The Poem of the Man God (The Gospel as revealed to me), first approved by Pope Pius XII in 1948, when in a meeting on February 26th 1948, witnessed by three other priests, he ordered the three priest present to "Publish this work as it is". In 1994, the Vatican heeded to the calls of Christians worldwide and have begun to examine the case for the Canonization of Maria Valtorta (Little John).

It is still the subject of much controversy, both rational and political, as are many great works. However, Faith is neither subject to rationalism nor to politics.

The Poem of the Man God was described by Pope Pius' confessor as "edifying". Mystical revelations have long been the province of priests and the religious. Now, they are accessible to all. May all who read this adaptation, which merges parts of the Mystical City of God and the Poem of the Man God, also find it edifying. Through this light, may Faith be renewed.

Special Thanks to the Centro Editoriale Valtortiano in Italy for permission to quote from the Poem of the Man God by Maria Valtorta, nick named, Little John.

Because I add no new material to these stories, I have chosen to remain anonymous.

"..May those be blessed who will accept the gift with simple hearts and faith. The fire which the Father wished today will light up in them. The world will not change in its cruelty. It is too corrupt. But they will be comforted and they will feel the thirst for God, the incentive to holiness, rise within themselves."

Jesus, 22nd February 1944.

The Flight to Egypt **9**

The Way to Egypt **22**

Jesus Breaks His Silence **32**

The Holy Family in Egypt **38**

Jesus' First Working Lesson **46**

The Return to Nazareth **50**

Mary Teaches Jesus, Judas and James. **55**

Preparations for Jesus' Coming of Age **70**

Jesus Examined at the Temple when He is of Age. **78**

Jesus Goes Missing In Jerusalem **89**

Jesus Disputes with the Doctors in the Temple **95**

The Flight to Egypt

Meanwhile, around the time of the visit of the Magi, Mary had begun a novena-a nine day prayer- of thanksgiving to God in memory of the nine months in which She bore Jesus in Her womb. On each day, She offered anew, Her Son to the eternal Father for the salvation of man. In answer to Her prayers and offerings, She receives many privileges from the Almighty; that as long as the world should last, all Her requests on behalf of Her clients shall be granted, through Her, all sinners shall find salvation, She shall be Co-Redeemer with Christ and many others.

But on the fifth day of this novena, whilst She prays, She receives an abstract vision of the Almighty in which He prepares Her for the trials that lay ahead:

"My Spouse and my Dove, your wishes and intentions are pleasing in my eyes and I delight in them always. But you cannot finish the nine days' devotion, which you have begun, for I have in store for you other exercises of your

love. In order to save the life of your Son and raise Him up, you must leave your home and your country; fly with Him and your spouse Joseph into Egypt, where you are to remain until I shall ordain otherwise: for Herod is seeking the life of the Child. The journey is long, most laborious and most fatiguing; do you suffer it all for my sake; for I am, and always will be, with you."

Answering, She says:

"My Lord and Master, behold your servant with a heart prepared to die for your love. Dispose of me according to your will. This only do I ask of your immense goodness, that, overlooking my want of merit and gratitude, You permit not my Son and Lord to suffer, and that You turn all pains and labour upon me, who am obliged to suffer them."

The Lord refers Her to Joseph, telling Her to follow his directions in all things concerning the journey.

She comes out of the vision, which She receives fully conscious and holding Jesus in Her arms, Her compassionate heart deeply harrowed at the thought of the difficulties ahead and She sheds many tears. Joseph perceives Her grief and is disturbed by it but out of humility and respect for Her spouse, She hides the cause of Her sorrow and says nothing of the vision, waiting for

Providence to take its course. That very same night an angel speaks to Joseph in His sleep.

It is night time, not long after the visit of the Magi. Joseph is fast asleep in his little bed, in his very small room- merely the size of a corridor- the sleep of a man after a hard day's diligent work. The shutters are ajar to let in the cool air and to wake him with the first rays of day break. A thin ray of moonlight filters in through the open shutters and shows him lying on his side, smiling at some vision he sees in his dream. An angel of the Lord speaks to him in his sleep:

"Arise, take the Child and its Mother and fly into Egypt; there you shall remain until I return to give you other advice; for Herod is seeking after the Child in order to take away its life"

Joseph's smile quickly turns into an expression of anxiety, he sighs deeply, as one who has had a nightmare and then wakes with a start.

He sits up in his bed, rubs his eyes and looks around, at the little window where the feeble light if filtering in. It is the dead of night but he grasps his robe from where it lay at the bottom of the bed and, still sitting on the bed, pulls it on over the white short-sleeved tunic he's wearing next to his skin. He detangles himself from the blanket, puts his feet on the floor, searches for his sandals, puts them on and ties the laces. Standing up, he lights a small oil lamp and then taking it with him, walks forward a few paces to the door facing his bed- not the one at the side of the bed that leads into the room where the magi were received.

Softly with his fingertips, he knocks, waits for an answer and then carefully opens the door, silently, ajar and enters. It's a slightly larger room with a low bed standing next to a cradle. The room is softly lit by a night lamp flickering like a distant star giving off a soft golden light.

Mary is kneeling by the cradle in a light dress, praying and watching Jesus, Who is sleeping peacefully, beautiful, rosy and fair haired, with his curly head sunk in the pillow and a fist clenched under His chin.

'Are You not sleeping?' Joseph asks in a low voice, somewhat surprised. 'Why not? Is Jesus not well?'

'Oh, No! He is all right. I am praying. Later, I will sleep. Why have you come, Joseph?' asks Mary, still kneeling.

'We must go away from here at once' says Joseph in an excited whisper. 'It must be at once. Prepare the coffer and a sack with everything You can put in them. I'll prepare the rest....I'll take as much as I can....we must flee at dawn. I would go sooner but I must speak to the landlady...'

'But why this flight?'

'I will tell you later. It's because of Jesus. An angel said to me: "Take the Child and His Mother and escape to Egypt." Don't waste any time. I'm going to prepare what I can.'

At the mention of Angel, Jesus and flight, Mary understands that Her Child is in danger, that the prophecy of Simeon is beginning to come true and springs to Her feet, Her face whiter then wax, holding one hand against Her heart in distress. Quick, light on Her feet and orderly, She places a large sack on Her bed and begins laying clothes both in a coffer and in the sack on Her bed. Although She is deeply distressed, She remains calm. Now and again, She looks at the Child sleeping calmly in the cradle as She passes by.

'Do you need help?' asks Joseph from time to time, peeping in through the door left ajar.

'No, thank you' answers Mary every time.

When the sack is full and obviously very heavy, Mary calls Joseph to help Her close it. Preferring to do it alone, Joseph carries the long sack into his little room.

'Shall I also take the woollen blankets?' asks Mary

'Take as much as you can. We will lose the rest. Do take as much as You can....Things will be useful because...because we will have to stay away for a long time, Mary!...' says Joseph sadly.

Mary sighs deeply as She folds Her blankets and Joseph's. ' We will leave the quilts and mats....' says Joseph whilst he ties the blankets with a rope. '... Even if I take three donkeys, I cannot overload them. We will have a long and uncomfortable journey....partly in the mountains and partly in the desert...Cover Jesus well...

....The nights will be cold both up in the mountains and in the desert.....I have taken the gifts of the Magi because they will be very useful down there. I am going to spend all the money I have to buy two donkeys. ....We cannot send them back so I will have to buy them.....I will go now, without waiting for dawn.....I know where to find them. ...You finish preparing everything.' and he goes out.

Mary gathers a few more things, looks at Jesus, then goes out and returns with some little dresses that appear damp; perhaps only washed the day before. She folds them then wraps them up in a cloth and adds them to the other things. There is nothing else.

She looks around one last time and, in a corner, sees one of Jesus' toys: a little carved wooden sheep, nibbled at the ears and with traces of Jesus's little teeth all over it. She picks it up, sobbing, kisses it and caresses the thing without value; a plain piece of wood of great sentimental value to Her because it tells Her of Joseph's love for Jesus and speaks to Her of Her Child. She adds it to the other things placed on the coffer.

Now, there really is nothing else.

It is time to prepare the Child.

She goes to the cradle and shakes it gently to wake Him up but He whimpers a little, turns around and continues to sleep. Mary pats His curls gently and Jesus opens His little mouth yawning.
Leaning forward, Mary kisses His cheek and Jesus opens His eyes, sees His Mummy , smiles and stretches His little Hands towards Her breast.
'Yes, love of Your Mummy. Yes, Your milk. Before the usual time...But You are always ready to suck Your Mummy's breast, My little holy Lamb!'

Jesus laughs and plays, kicking His little feet out of the blanket, moving His arms happily in a typical childish fashion, so beautiful to see. He pushes His feet against His Mummy's stomach and arches His back leaning His fair head forward on Her breast and then throws Himself back and laughs, holding the laces that tie His Mother's dress to Her neck in His hands, trying to open it. He looks most beautiful in His little linen shirt, plump and as rosy as a flower.

Bending down and looking through the cradle as though for protection, She cries and smiles at the same time, whilst the Child prattles, uttering words which are not the words of all little children; among which the word "Mummy" is repeated very clearly. Surprised to see Her crying, He stretches out one little hand towards the shiny traces of tears, getting His hand wet as He pats Her face. Then, very, gracefully, He leans, once again, on His Mother's breast, clinging to it, patting it with His hand. His little woollen dress has now been put on Him and His sandals have been tied on His feet.

She nurses Him and Jesus sucks avidly at His Mother's good milk. When He feels that only a little is coming from Her right breast, He looks for the left one, laughing and looking up at His Mother as he does so.
Then He falls asleep again on Her breast, His rosy round little cheek resting against Her white round breast.

Slowly, Mary rises, gently lays Him down on the quilt on Her bed and covers Him with Her mantle. Then She goes back to the cradle and folds its little blankets.

Mary gets up obediently and puts on Her mantle whilst Joseph makes a last parcel and goes out with it.

Mary lifts the Child gently, envelops Him in a shawl and clasps Him to Her heart. She looks at the walls that have been home for Her for some months and touches them caressingly with one hand. Happy house that deserved to be loved and blessed by Mary!

She goes out, through Joseph's room, into the big room, where the landlady, in tears, kisses Her goodbye and, lifting the edge of the shawl, kisses the forehead of Jesus, Who is sleeping calmly. They go down the outside steps.

In the dim first light of dawn, three donkeys can be seen; the strongest is loaded with the goods and chattels. The other two are saddled.
Joseph is busy fastening the coffer and bundles on the pack saddle of the first one. His carpenter's tools are tied in a bundle on top of the sack.

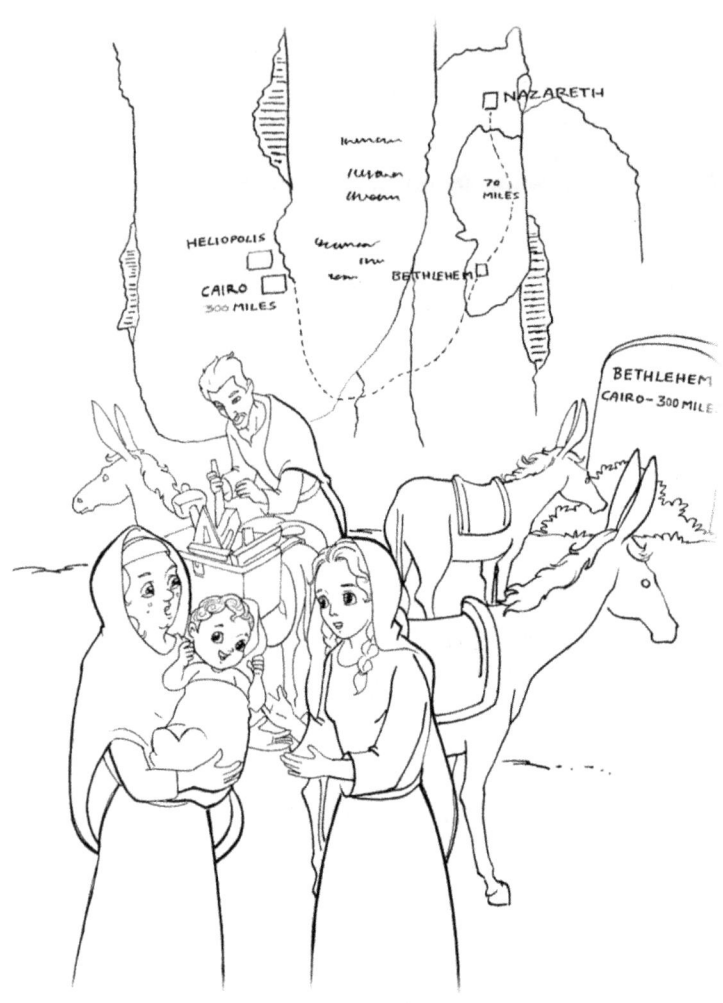

There are more tears and goodbyes and then Mary mounts the little donkey whilst the landlady, holding Jesus in her arms, kisses Him again. Then she hands Him back to

Mary.

Joseph ties his donkey to the one loaded with goods in order to be free to hold the reins of Mary's donkey. Finally, he mounts.

It is sometime around 9BC and Jesus is not yet one year old. The flight begins whilst Bethlehem sleeps peacefully unaware of the danger impending on it, perhaps still dreaming of the phantasmagoric scene of the visit of the Magi.

An angel appears to the returning Magi and warns them of the wicked intentions of Herod, who foolishly fearing that Jesus would deprive him of his kingdom, intends to find and kill the Messiah. Once again, the star appears and guides them away from Herod's palace and back to where they had met beyond the Dead Sea from where they go their separate ways. When Herod finds he has been deceived, he orders the massacre of all infants in the neighbourhood of Bethlehem.

The Way to Egypt

Through obedience, Providence has pre- arranged that come this day of flight, the holy family shall have to depart from Judea and not from Nazareth.

Escaping in the silence and darkness of night, Mary and Joseph have much to worry about as they know not what will happen on their journey, when it would end, how they would fare in Egypt being complete strangers, what means they would find there to raise the Child or even how they will protect Him during the crossing. They have three hundred miles to journey to their destination in Egypt, two hundred of those in the open desert in wintry conditions. Nevertheless, Mary is determined not to resort to the use of miracles for their needs, for as long as they can provide for themselves by their own effort.

They are accompanied by the ten thousand angels visible to them in human form, who offer homage and service, and inform that it is God's will that they guide and accompany Her on the journey. At once, they head for the Bersabe desert, stopping in Gaza for two days to rest themselves and their donkeys. From the early days of Jesus, news of repeated miracles wherever Christ went has drawn the attention of crowds and of those in power, making it easy for Herod and his men to quickly find the Infant God-Man.

During the two days' rest, they perform many miracles; many illnesses are cured, some sick are saved from the danger of death, a crippled woman gets back the use of her limbs ad many souls are revived but Mary and Joseph do not reveal who they are, where they come from nor where they're headed least the news should go back to Herod.

On the third day, they set of again and soon passed beyond the inhabited parts of Palestine and into the sandy Bersabe desert in which they are to journey for sixty leagues before they reach their final destination in Egypt.

God permits his Onlybegotten, with his most holy Mother and Joseph, to suffer the inconveniences and hardships naturally connected with travel through this desert and they bear their hardships without complaint although they are especially grieved for not being able to ease, by their own efforts, the hardships of their Son. They can only cover a short distance each day and the crossing lasts thirty days because of the difficulty of crossing the deep sands in addition to which they suffer from a lack of shelter particularly at night in the wintry conditions that already prevail in the desert by day and plummet by night.

One the first night, they rest at the foot of a small hill; the only protection they can find.

With the Child in Her arms, Mary sits Herself on the ground with Joseph and they share a sparse meal of fruit and bread acquired during their two days' rest, and Mary nurses Jesus at Her breast. Jesus, for His part, makes Mary and Joseph happy by His contentment.

Joseph builds a narrow tent with his cloak and some sticks as a makeshift shelter against the open air for Mary and Jesus whilst he sleeps on the ground with his head resting on the coffer and thus they pass their first night in the freezing desert, closely guarded by the angels.

Mary perceives Her divine Son offer all their hardships to the eternal Father and She joins Him for the greater part of the night, permitting themselves only a short sleep.

But their little store of fruit and bread soon runs out very early on and hunger sets in. A few days into the desert they have to travel all day without food until nine O'clock at night. With no means to provide for themselves, Mary prays to the eternal Father saying:

"Eternal, great and powerful God, I give You thanks and bless You for Your magnificent bounty; and that, by Your merciful condescension, without my merit, You gave me life and being and preserve me in it, though I am but dust and a useless creature. I have not made a proper return for all these benefits; therefore how can I ask for myself what I cannot repay? But, my Lord and Father, look upon Your Onlybegotten and grant me what is necessary to sustain my natural life and that of my spouse, so that I may serve Your Majesty and Your Word made flesh for the salvation of men."

So that the clamours of the sweetest Mother might proceed from yet greater suffering, the Most High permits the elements to afflict them more than is usual, adding to the sufferings caused by their fatigue and hunger so that listening to the acceptable prayers of his Spouse, He might make provision also for these by the hands of the angels. And so a furious storm with lashing wind and rain rises, harassing and blinding them.

Mary wraps Jesus up and tries to protect Him as much as She can but Her tender heart grieves deeply as Jesus, delicate as He is, weeps and shivers from the stormy weather.

Finally, Mary uses Her power as the Mother of God, commanding the elements not to afflict Her Son but rather to afford Him shelter and refreshment and wreak their vengeance upon Her alone. The storm abates immediately, sparing both Mother and Child.

In return for this loving forethought, the Infant Jesus commands his angels to assist His kindest Mother against the storm. They immediately build a beautiful globe about and over their Incarnate God, His Mother and Her spouse and thus protect and defend them for the rest of the journey through the desert.

They also bring them delicious bread, seasoned fruits and a most delicious drink which they serve themselves. And then, together, the angels and the holy Family sing and give praise and thanksgiving to God. And for the rest of their journey through the desert, God provides them with their food.

Upon arrival in Egypt, they find a people held captive by the Evil One. The Infant Jesus, in His Mother's arms, raises His eyes and His hands to the Father asking for their salvation, thus driving demons from idols, hurling them back into the caverns and darkness of hell, idols crash to the ground, altars fall to pieces and temples crumble to ruins. Mary unites Her prayers to the prayers of Her Son and Joseph is aware of the works of the Incarnate Word but the Egyptian people are astonished. Though the learned amongst them remember an ancient tradition prophesied by Isaiah (Is.9,1) which tells of the arrival of a King of the Jews and the destruction of the temples of idols, they did not know how this prophesy is to be fulfilled.

The people who speak to Mary and Joseph, come to them out of curiosity at seeing strangers in their midst and speaking, express their fears at the recent happenings but Mary and Joseph use the occasion to speak to them at length about the one true God, Creator or heaven and earth, Who alone is to be acknowledged and adored.

Mary is so sweet and charming and Her words so kind that rumour quickly spreads of the arrival of strange pilgrims whilst the prayers of the Incarnate Word, converts the hearts of many, instilling the knowledge of God and sorrow for their sins, which together with the destruction of idols, causes an incredible commotion but the people do not know from Whom the blessings come.

Jesus, Mary and Joseph pursue their journey through

Memphis, Babylon, Matarieh to Heliopolis (present day: Mit Rahina, 12 miles south of Cairo, Coptic Cairo, five miles north east of Cairo, north-east edge of Cairo respectively), working miracles, casting demons out of people and idols, curing the sick and enlightening hearts on the doctrines of eternal life. In Heliopolis, they are informed by the angels that they are to stay there. Joseph buys a house, a poor dwelling with three rooms just outside the City as Mary desires. One room is assigned as the temple of Jesus in which they place His cradle and Mary's couch. The second is assigned to Joseph and the third serves both as Kitchen and workshop for Joseph.

True to Her resolve to provide for Her family by Her own labour, Mary immediately sets about looking for needlework through the help of the pious women drawn to Her modesty and sweetness. The reputation of Her skill and diligent work soon spreads and She gets so much work that She allots Her days to working and Her nights to Her spiritual exercises even though She continues Her spiritual meditations whilst she works. Thus Joseph and Mary together are able to provide for all the basic needs of food and clothing for their Child and themselves.

Illness and disease are prevalent in Egypt because of the harsh climate and many who come to Mary to hear the word of God return home cured, in body and soul. So word quickly spreads. To make matters worse, Heliopolis and many other parts of Egypt are ravaged by pestilence during the years of their stay so at Mary's request, Jesus ordains Joseph; giving him new light and the power to heal. So whilst Joseph teaches and heals the men, Mary, attends to the women and all who come to them receive grace and are moved with love and devotion at the modesty and holiness of Mary. But She refuses payment or presents offered except where She finds the present useful to help another in need in which case She also makes a return present of Her needlework.

Through Her work in spreading the word of God in Egypt and helping the Egyptians in body and soul, Mary Herself grows in sanctity. God gives Her full knowledge-as though She Herself had been present- of the massacre of the innocents- all first born sons of one day old to two years old- by Herod in his search for the Messiah She knows all this as if She Herself had been present.

Through Her prayers and those of Her son, all these innocents receive high knowledge of the being of God, of perfect love, faith and hope with which they immediately put to use, performing heroic acts of faith, love and worship of God and receive God's compassion for their parents and families, obtaining, light and grace in advance in spiritual needs. Notwithstanding their tender age, these children willingly submit to martyrdom thus increasing their merits and are borne to limbo by a multitude of angels to await the redemption. Their arrival in limbo in turn reaffirms the ancients of the hope of a speedy liberation for which there is much rejoicing and songs of praise. All this, Mary does in union with Her divine Child Who is the author of them all, but Who, whilst in Egypt, must remain as normal to all else.

Jesus Breaks His Silence

One day, Mary and Joseph are conversing and reflecting on the infinite being of God, His goodness and excessive love that induced Him to send His Onlybegotten Son to be the Teacher and Saviour of men, God clothed in flesh, come to converse with mankind and suffer the punishment of their depraved natures. As he reflects, Joseph's heart inflames with love and he is lost in wonder and awe of God's works.

Jesus, in His Mother's arms, has just turned one year old and He seizes this opportunity to break His silence to Joseph. 'My father...' He says to Joseph '..... I am the Light of the World, come from Heaven to rescue the world from the darkness of sin, as a good Shepherd, to teach My sheep the way of Salvation and open the gates of Heaven closed by sin. I desire that you both be children of Light, which you have so close at hand.'

His words fill Joseph with new reverence and joy, and throwing himself upon his knees before the infant God, he thanks Him for having called him "father" for Joseph loves Jesus with an exquisite supernatural love far higher than the natural love of any earthly father for his son.

Joseph is humbled to hear himself called 'father' by the Son of the eternal Father, the Son Whom he sees so beautiful in grace and exalted in knowledge and wisdom.

From the time that Jesus is a year old, He begins to spend certain hours of the day in His chapel and, responding to His Mother's mute appeal, invites Her to join Him so that She might learn from Him and imitate Him in His works as He wishes Her to be the model of perfect accomplishment for all souls. And so Jesus, from this time - in Egypt, through to their return to Nazareth and up to the start of his ministry-teaches Mary, by word of mouth all the mysteries of the evangelical law and of his doctrine upon which he will found His Church on earth, pointing out the time and place of each event, and the timeline of the kingdoms and provinces during the life of the Church. After their return to Nazareth following the ceremony of Jesus' coming of age, Jesus also teaches Mary the secrets of the book with seven Seals of which John speaks (Apoc. 5,1); the book that only the Lamb can unseal by His Passion and Death, His doctrines and merits. In comparison, Jesus spends only three years to teach His Apostles and His Disciples and fully establish His Church on earth.

Sometimes during their teachings and prayers, Jesus is prostrate on the ground, at other times, He is raised from the ground, always in the form of a cross, praying earnestly to the eternal Father for the salvation of mortal souls. Often, in the presence of Mary, He would say;

'O most blessed Cross! When shall your arms receive mine, when shall I rest on you, when shall my arms, nailed to yours be spread to welcome all sinners? .....As I have come for no other purpose than to invite them to imitate Me....they are even now and forever open to embrace and enrich all men. Come then, all you that are blind, to the light. Come you poor, to the treasures of my grace. Come, you little ones, to the caresses and delights of your true Father. Come, you afflicted and worn out, for I will relieve and refresh you.....

Come, you just, since you are my possession and inheritance. Come all you children of Adam, for I call upon you all. I am the way, the truth and the life and I will deny nothing that you desire to receive...... My eternal Father, they are the works of Your hands, do not despise them; for I will offer Myself as a sacrifice on the Cross, in order to restore them to justice and freedom. If they be but willing I will lead them back to the bosom of Your elect and to their heavenly kingdom, where Your name shall be glorified."

And Mary joins Her prayers to His for She is made aware of what transpires in His soul as well as what She observes as the external movements of His body. As such, even though Mary does not always enjoy visions of the Divinity, it is a privilege reserved only for Her that through Her Son, She is made aware of all their activities and the way in which His humanity reveres, loves and adores the Divinity to which it is united. In this special manner, She is witness to the effects of the hypostatic union of the humanity with the Divinity-the Man-God.

In is temple, Jesus confers with His Father about the highest mysteries of the Redemption, and the Person of the Father approves or concedes to His petitions for the relief of men, or shows the humanity of Christ the secret decrees of the doctrine that God has ordained all that will happen with regard to the salvation of some and not others, the condemnation of some souls to eternal misery. All this, Mary is witness to, adoring the Omnipotent with unequalled reverence and joining Her Son in His payers, petitions and thanksgiving.

On some such occasions, the Child weeps and perspires blood, and this will happen many times both in Egypt and after their return to Nazareth, long before that recorded in the garden of Gethsemane. At such times, Mary wipes His face, fully understanding the cause of His agony to be the loss of the foreknown; those for whom the merits of the Redeemer will be wasted.

At other times, Jesus is transfigured by the overflow of the glory of His most holy soul into the body so that he is shrouded in heavenly light because the eternal Father ordained that the divine humanity should at intervals, have this consolation. At such, and at other times when Jesus is not glorified, He is surrounded by angels singing sweet hymns of praise in celestial harmony. And Mary joins in the hymns of praise.

The children of Heliopolis who play with Child Jesus, free from great malice as most children are, accept Him as He is and Jesus, accepts them in return as far as is befitting, instils in them knowledge of God and of virtues, teaches them the way of eternal life, impresses His truths deeply upon them and wins their hearts so that all of them who have this good fortune, afterwards become great saintly men as in the course of time, these seeds of grace sown early in their souls, ripen and bear heavenly fruits.

The Holy Family in Egypt

Two year old Jesus is sitting on a mat in the shade of a small tree that stands at the centre of a kitchen garden within a small enclosed piece of ground. The arid garden soil has been patiently cultivated and hedged in with cane, fortified with creepers, modest convolvuli, and on one side, a shrub of jasmine in full bloom and a bush of common roses. Some modest vegetables are growing in the centre of the garden, under the tree, where there is some shade. A little black and white goat tied to the tree, is browsing on the leaves of some branches thrown on the grown.

The garden belongs to a small poor house with plastered walls and a single floor- ground floor-. The walls are whitewashed and there are two doors, one near the other, that lead to the inner rooms of the little house. The house stands in the middle of the small piece of sandy ground enclosed with the weak fence made with cane fixed to the ground, suitable protection only against stray dogs and cats.

On His mat in the grounds of the poor house, Jesus is playing with little wooden sheep, little wooden horses and some clear wooden shavings, less curly than His golden curls. With His little plum hands, He is trying to put wooden necklaces onto the necks of His animals. He is quiet, smiling and very beautiful. His little head is a mass of very thick little golden curls, His skin, clear and slightly rosy. His eyes, alive and a deep bright blue; two beautiful dark sapphires. He is wearing a white tunic reaching to His calves, with short sleeves and tied at the waist with a white cord. His tiny feet are bare because He has taken off His sandals and is using them as a cart for his animals, pulling the cart by the straps.

The sandals are simple; a sole and two straps, one from the point and the other from the heel. The one from the point splits in two at a certain point and one length then passes through an eyelet in the strap from the heel, then goes round and is tied with the other piece thus forming a ring at the ankle.

Also in the shade of the tree, not far from Jesus, is Mary, weaving at a rustic loom and watching the Child. Her white slender hand moves forwards and backwards, throwing the shuttle on the weft while Her sandaled foot moves the pedal. Her tunic is the colour of mallow flowers: a rosy violet like certain amethysts. She is bareheaded and Her hair is parted into two simple braids gathered at the nape of Her neck. Her sleeves are long and narrow and She wears no other ornament but Her beauty and most sweet expression in Her face of a blue angel, that looks about twenty years old.

Her day's work done, She gets up and bending over the Child, puts His sandals back on and ties the laces carefully. Then She pats Him and kisses His beautiful eyes. The Child prattles and She answers Him. Then, going back to Her loom, She covers the fabric and the weft with a piece of cloth, picks up the stool She was sitting on and takes it into the house. The Child follows Her with His eyes but does not mind being left alone.

The sun is setting over the barren sands and a huge fire invades the whole sky behind the distant pyramid.

Mary comes back and taking Jesus by the hand, lifts Him from His mat. The Child obeys without resistance. While His Mother gathers His toys and takes them into the house, He toddles over, on His shapely little legs, to the goat and throws His arms around its neck. The little goat bleats and rubs its head on Jesus' shoulder.

Mary comes back, now wearing a veil and carrying an amphora in Her hand. She takes Jesus by the hand and, together, they walk gracefully round the little house, a pretty picture. Mary adjusts Her steps to the Child's and the Child toddles and trips along beside Her, His rosy heels moving up and down on the sandy path with the typical grace of children's steps.

At the front of the house, the hedge is broken by a rustic gate which Mary opens to go out onto the road, a poor road at the end of the village, leading into the country made of sand and other poor houses similar to theirs, and with scanty gardens.

There is no one about. Mary looks towards the town as if She is expecting someone and then directs Her steps towards a well surrounded by some herbs on the ground and inside a circle of shade provided by palm trees some ten meters ahead.

There's a man walking down the road. In the distance, he is not very tall but well built. As he draws closer, his features emerge and it is Joseph, smiling. He looks in his mid-thirties, his hair and beard thick and black, his skin rather tanned, his eyes dark, his honest face inspiring confidence.

When he sees Jesus and Mary, he quickens his step. He is carrying his saw and plane on his left shoulder and other tools of his trade in his other hand, perhaps returning from a house call. His tunic of a workman is between hazel and dark brown in colour and it reaches his calves, has short sleeves and is held at the waist with a leather belt. His sandals are tied at the ankles.

Mary smiles and Jesus utters a cry of joy, stretching out His free hand. When they meet, Mary takes Joseph's work tools and Joseph bends down offering Jesus a fruit. Then, crouching to the ground, he stretches his arms and Jesus leaves His Mother and cuddles in Joseph's arms, bending His little head into the cavity of Joseph's neck. Joseph kisses Him and is kissed by Him, a scene full of loving grace.

Then Joseph stands up and takes his tools with his left

hand whilst with his right he clasps Jesus tight to his strong chest. Then he goes back with Jesus to the house whilst Mary goes to the well to fill Her amphora.

Inside the grounds of the house, Joseph puts the Child down and carry's Mary's loom into the house. Then he milks the goat and then takes it into its little closet by the house whilst Jesus watches keenly.

It is now getting dark as the red sunset turns to violet on the sands that seem to tremble from the heat, and on the pyramid making it look darker.

Joseph goes into the house, into a room that is his workshop, kitchen and dining room all in one. There's a fire lit in the low fireplace. There's a carpenter's bench, a small table, some stools and some shelves with two lamps and some kitchenware on them. Mary's loom is in the corner. The house, though poor, is orderly and very clean.

Mary comes back with the amphora and they close the door on the rapidly growing darkness outside. The room is illuminated by a lamp which Joseph has lit and placed on his bench, where he is now working on some small boards whilst Mary prepares supper. The fire in the fireplace also lights the room. Jesus, with His little hands placed on the bench and His little head raised upwards, is keenly watching Joseph at work.

They come to the table and Joseph leads them in a psalm in their dialect of Nazareth whilst Mary answers. They sit down to eat with the lamp on the table and Jesus on Mary's lap. Mary makes Him drink some goat's milk. Then She cuts some slices of bread from a round brown loaf of bread, dips them in the milk and offers them to Jesus. Joseph eats a small slice of cheese and a lot of bread. Mary sits Jesus on a stool near Her and fetches some cooked vegetables- they are boiled and dressed, and when Joseph has helped himself, Mary also has some, whilst Jesus nibbles happily at His apple, smiling and displaying His little white teeth.
They finish their supper with some hard dates and there is no wine. The super of poor people.

But there is much peace in the room.

Jesus' First Working Lesson

A little five year old boy, completely blond and most beautiful in a simple blue tunic reaching half way down his shapely calves, is playing with some earth in the little kitchen garden of their home; He makes little heaps with the earth and plants little branches on top to make a miniature forest. Then He builds little roads with stone and now, He would like to build a little lake at the foot of His tiny hills. So He takes the bottom part of an old pot and bury's it up to the brim then He fills it with water using a pitcher which He dips in a vessel containing water used for washing and for watering the little garden, wetting His dress and sleeves. But the chipped pot is also cracked and the lake dries up.

Joseph comes to the door and stands there for some time quietly watching Jesus at work and smiling.

Then to prevent Jesus from getting Himself more wet, he calls Him. Jesus turns round smiling and when He sees Joseph, He runs to him with His little arms outstretched.

With the edge of his work tunic, Joseph dries His little hands which are soiled and wet, and kisses them. And then, the two have a conversation in which Jesus explains His game, His work and the difficulties He is having; He wanted to make a little lake like the lake of Gennesaret- that He has heard spoken of-, a little one for His own delight. This was Tiberias, there was Magdala, over there was Capernaum. This was the road to Nazareth going through Cana. He wanted to launch some little boats in the lake; these leaves are the boats. And He wanted to go over to the other shore. But the water runs away...

Joseph watches and takes an interest as if it were a very serious matter. Then he proposes to make a small lake the next day, not with an old cracked pot, but with a small wooden basin, well coated with pitch and stucco, in which Jesus would launch small real wooden boats which he, Joseph, will teach Him how to make. Just then, he had brought Him some small working tools, suitable for Him, so He might learn to use them without any fatigue.

'So I will be able to help you!' says Jesus, smiling.

'So You will help me and You will become a clever carpenter. Come and see them.'

They go into the workshop and Joseph shows Him a small hammer, a tiny saw, some very small chisels and a plane suitable for a doll, all laid out on a small workbench of a budding carpenter; suitable for little Jesus' size.

'See, to saw, You must put this piece of wood like that. You then take the saw like that, and making sure not to catch Your fingers, You start sawing. Try...'

And the lesson begins. And Jesus, blushing with the effort and pressing His lips together, saws the piece of wood carefully and then planes it and although it isn't perfectly straight, He thinks it is nice. Joseph praises Him and with patience and love, teaches Him how to work.

Mary, returning from an errand, looks in at the door and smiles at the zeal with which Jesus is working with the plane and at how lovingly Joseph is teaching Him.
Sensing Her presence, Jesus turns round and runs to Her to show Her the little piece of wood not yet finished. Mary admires it, then bends down and kisses Jesus. She tidies His ruffled curls, wipes the perspiration from His hot face and listens with loving attention to Jesus, Who promises to make Her a little stool so that She will be more comfortable when working. Joseph, standing near the tiny bench with one hand resting on his side, looks on and smiles.

The Return to Nazareth

The decree for the departure from Egypt, over four years since they first arrived, is intimated by the eternal Father to His Son in the presence of His Mother. Mary sees it mirrored in His most holy soul and also sees Him submit in obedience to the father. But neither Mother nor Son make this known to Joseph, because although Jesus is true God and His Mother highly exalted above Joseph, God places great value in the proper order of created things and thus the arrangements for the journey must proceed from Joseph as the head of the Family.
That same night, an angel speaks to Joseph in his sleep, telling him to take the Child and His Mother and return to the land of Israel because Herod and those who with him had sought the life of the Child, were dead.

There is much distress and much sorrow amongst their friends and acquaintances who sigh, complain loudly and weep on account of the great loss of their benefactress. The holy family depart for Palestine in the company of the angels as on their outbound journey and everywhere they pass, they scatter graces and blessings; the news of their passage once more drawing crowds of the sick and afflicted who all find relieve in body and soul as many are cured, demons expelled and souls enlightened.

They find their home in Nazareth, having been left in the charge of Joseph's cousin, in good condition.

Mary enters and immediately prostrates Herself in adoration of the Lord and in thanksgiving for having led them to safety from the cruelty of Herod, preserved them from the dangers of their long and arduous journeys and their banishment and then for having returned them safely to their home, in the company of Her Son, now grown in years, grace and virtue.

Once again, they set up home, ordering their lives so that Mary continues to receive instruction from Her Son and caring for Him and for Her Spouse whilst Joseph works to earn sustenance for Jesus and Mary as head of the family.

Shortly after their return to Nazareth, Jesus resolves to try the strength of Mary's love and of all Her virtues, in order to raise the level of Mary's holiness to be second only to that of God. Suddenly, without warning, He becomes reserved, withdraws Himself from Her interior sight, suspends His tokens of affection for Her, withdrawing also from her company and although he remains physically present, He speaks only the occasional word to Her and even then, with great Majesty.

This unexpected change is the forge in which the purest gold of Mary's love for Her Lord is once again purified, as Her heart, as one stricken with an arrow, is wrenched with grief. Having received no explanation for this behaviour, surprised at it and not knowing what might be its cause, Mary takes refuge in Her humility and attributing these actions to Her ingratitude and other shortfalls on Her part. She is filled with dread not so much at the privation of his delightful graces but for having fallen short in His service and thus displeased Him. She performs heroic acts of all the virtues, humbling Herself below the dust, adoring Her Son, thanking the eternal Father for His admirable works and blessings, seeking to know His will in order to fulfil it in all things, constantly renewing Her acts of faith, hope and love, persevering in tearful prayers pouring forth Her grief before the throne of God.

Her loving sighs and tender affection wound His heart but He maintains His external reserve, avoiding Her every time She seeks Him out to converse with Him. Such avoidance only intensifies Her grief and causes Her to seek Him more and this goes on for thirty days- equal to many ages in the estimation of Her who deems it impossible to live even for one moment without Her Beloved- so that the flame of love in Her heart is fanned to an intense blaze.

The loving Mother eventually approaches and throws Herself at Her Son's feet adoring and begging His forgiveness saying;

'My sweetest love and highest Good.....If I have not been zealous in serving You, as I am constrained to confess, do chastise my negligence and pardon it. But let me, my Son and Lord, see the gladness of Your countenance, which is my salvation and the light of my life. Here at Your feet I lay my poverty, mingling it with the dust, and I shall not rise from it until I can again look into the mirror, which reflects my soul.'

The heart of the Child, Jesus, after the thirty days, can no longer resist the immense force of His love for His sweetest Mother for He also suffers a wonderful violence in holding Her at a distance.

"My Mother, arise." Jesus says, simply but at His words, Mary is uplifted into ecstasy, Her vision of the Divinity is restored and She sees the Lord receive Her with the sweetest embrace of welcome of a Father and Spouse, Her tears are turned to rejoicing, Her suffering to delight, Her bitterness into highest sweetness.

Mary Teaches Jesus, Judas and James.

The sounds of Joseph working in his workshop in Nazareth drift into the silence of the dining room where Mary is sewing some strips of wool She has woven Herself. The strips are about a meter and a half by three meters long, from which She plans to make a mantle for Joseph.

Ruffled hedges of little violet blue daisies in full bloom can be seen through the open door that leads into the kitchen garden, announcing autumn, although the plants in the garden are still thick and beautiful with green foliage.

Bees from two beehives leaning against a sunny wall are flying about in the bright sunshine, buzzing and dancing from the fig tree to the vines and then to the pomegranate tree laden with round fruits, some of which have already burst open from excessive growth, baring the strings of juicy rubies lined up inside the green-red caskets partitioned into yellow sections.

Jesus, His little blond head like a blaze of light, is playing under the trees with two boys His cousins James and Judas, who are about His own age. They have curly hair, but they are not blond.

One, on the contrary, has very dark curls that make his little round face seem whiter, and two most beautiful large, wide open blue violet eyes.

The other is less curly and his hair is dark brown, his eyes also brown and his complexion darker, with a pinkish hue on his cheeks.

The three children are playing shops in perfect harmony with little carts on which there are various articles: leaves, little stones, wood shavings, little pieces of wood.

Jesus is the one who buys things for His Mummy, to Whom He takes now one thing, then another one. Mary accepts all the purchases with a smile.

Then the game changes. James, one of the two cousins proposes: ' Let us play at the Exodus from Egypt. Jesus will be Moses, I will be Aaron, and you... Mary. '

'But I am a boy! ' protests Judas.

'It does not matter. It's just the same. You are Mary, and you shall dance before the golden calf, and the golden calf is that beehive over there. '

'I'm not going to dance. I am a man and I do not want to be a woman. I am a faithful believer and I am not going to dance before an idol. '

Jesus interrupts them: 'Don't let us play that part. Let us play this other one: when Joshua is elected Moses' successor. So there will be no terrible sin of idolatry and Judas will be happy to be a man and My successor. Are you happy?'

' Yes I am, Jesus. But then You will have to die, because Moses dies afterwards. But I do not want You to die; You have always been so fond of me.'

'Everybody dies... but before dying I shall bless Israel, and since you are the only ones here, I shall bless the whole of Israel in you. '

They agree. Then there is an argument: whether the people of Israel, after so much travelling, still had the same carts which they had when leaving Egypt. There is a difference of opinion.

They apply to Mary. 'Mummy, I say that the Israelites still had the carts. James says they didn't. Judas does not know. Who is right. Do you know? '

' Yes, My Son. The nomadic people still had their carts. They repaired them when they stopped to rest. The weaker people travelled in them and also the foodstuffs and the many things which were necessary for so many people were loaded into them. With the exception of the Ark, which was carried by hand, everything else was on the carts. '

The question now answered, the children go down to the bottom of the orchard and from there, singing psalms, they come towards the house with Jesus in the lead singing psalms in His gentle silvery voice, followed by Judas and James holding a little cart elevated to the rank of Tabernacle.

But since they also have to play the part of the people, in addition to Aaron's and Joshua's, with their belts they have tied other miniature carts to their feet and thus they proceed very seriously, like real actors.

They complete the full length of the pergola and as they pass in front of the door of Mary's room, Jesus says:

'Mummy, hail the Ark when it passes by. '
Mary stands up smiling, and She bows to Her Son Who passes by, radiant in the bright sunshine.

Then Jesus clambers up the side of the mountain that forms the outer boundary of the garden, stands upright on top of the little grotto, and speaks to... Israel, repeating the orders and the promises of God. Then He appoints Joshua leader, calls him, and then Judas in his turn climbs up the cliff. Jesus-Moses encourages and blesses Judas-Joshua ....and then He asks for a... tablet (a large fig leaf), writes the canticle and reads it.
It is not quite complete, but contains a large part of it, and He seems to be reading it from the leaf. Then He dismisses Judas-Joshua who embraces Him crying. Jesus-Moses then climbs further up, right up to the edge of the cliff and from there, blesses the whole of Israel, that is the two who are prostrated on the ground. He then lies down on the short grass, closes His eyes and... dies.

When She sees Him lying still on the ground, Mary, who has been watching from the doorstep smiling, shouts: ' Jesus, Jesus! Get up! Don't lie down like that! Your Mummy does not want to see You dead! '

Jesus gets up smiling, runs towards Her, and kisses Her. James and Judas also come down and receive Mary's caresses.

'How can Jesus remember that canticle that is so long and difficult and all those blessings? 'Asks James.

Mary smiles and answers: 'His memory is very good and He pays a lot of attention when I read. '

'I too, at school, pay attention. But then I get sleepy with all the hubbub... shall I never learn then? '

'You will learn, be good. '

There's a knock at the door and Joseph quickly walks across the orchard and the house and opens it.

'Peace to you, Alphaeus and Mary' Joseph greets his brother and sister-in-law, who have left their rustic cart and healthy looking donkey waiting in the street outside.

'And to you, and blessings!'

'Did you have a good trip?'
'Very good. And the children?'
'They are in the garden with Mary.'

But the children have come to greet their mother. And so has Mary, holding Jesus by the hand. The two sisters-in-law kiss each other.

'Have they been good?' asks Mary of Alphaeus

'Very good and very dear' answers Mary. 'Are the relatives all well?'

'Yes, they all are. They send You their regards. And they have sent You many presents from Cana; grapes, apples, cheese, eggs, honey......
And...,Joseph?....I have found just what you wanted for Jesus. It is in the cart, in the round basket.' adds Mary of Alphaeus, bending over Jesus, Who is looking at her with His eyes wide open.
'.......Do you know what I have for You? .....Guess.' she asks, kissing His two strips of blue sky.

Jesus thinks, but He cannot guess......perhaps deliberately so as to give Joseph the joy of giving Him a surprise. Joseph, in fact, comes in, carrying a large round basket, lays it down on the floor in front of Jesus and unties the rope holding the lid in place and lifts it....and a little white sheep, a real flock of foam, appears, sleeping in the clean hay.

'Oh!' exclaims Jesus, joyfully surprised and happy. He's about to rush to the little animal but then turns round and runs to Joseph, who is still bending down over the basket, kisses and thanks him.

The two little cousins look with admiration at the little creature, which is now awake and lifting its little rosy head, bleating, looking for its mother. They carry it out of the basket and offer it a handful of clover and it browses, looking around with its mild eyes.

'For Me! For Me! Thank you father!' sings Jesus joyfully.

'Do you like it so much!'

'Oh! Very much!' White, clean....a little lamb....Oh!' And He throws His little arms around the sheep's neck, lays His blond head on its little head and remains thus, happy.

'I brought two more, also for you' says Alphaeus to his sons. 'But they are dark. You are not quite so tidy as Jesus and your sheep would always be untidy if they were white. They will be your herd; you will keep them together and so you will no longer loiter in the streets, you two little rascals, throwing stones at each other.'

Judas and James both run to the cart and look at the other two little sheep, which are more black than white, whilst Jesus takes his sheep into the garden, gives it some water to drink and the little pet follows Him as if it had known Him forever. Jesus beckons to it and calls it "Snow" and the sheep bleats happily in answer.

The guests sit at the table and Mary offers them some bread, some olives, some cheese and a jug of liquid of a very pale colour which might be cider or some water sweetened with honey.

The adults converse whilst the three boys play with their pets that Jesus wants gathered together so He can give them water and a name.
'Yours, Judas, will be called "Star" because it has that mark on its forehead.......And the name of yours will be "Flame" because it has the blazing colours of certain withering heathers.'

'Agreed.'

The adults are talking and Alphaeus says 'I hope I have solved the matter of the boys' quarrels. I got the idea from your request, Joseph. I said to myself: "My brother wants a little sheep for Jesus so He may have something to play with. I will get two more for those naughty boys to keep them quiet a little and avoid continuous arguments with other parents over bruised heads and skinned knees....with the school and with the sheep, I will manage to keep them quiet." But this year, You also, will have to send Jesus to school. It is time'

'I will never send Jesus to school.' says Mary resolutely. It is quite unusual to hear Her talk thus and even more so, to hear Her talk before Joseph.

'Why? The Child must learn to be ready in good time to pass His exam when He comes of age...'

'The Child will be ready. But He will not go to school. That is quite definite.'

'You will be the only woman in Israel to do that.'

'I will be the only one. But that is what I am going to do. Isn't that right Joseph.'

'Yes, that's correct. There is no need for Jesus to go to school. Mary was brought up in the Temple and She knows the law as well as any Doctor. She will be His Teacher. That's what I want too.'

'You are spoiling the Boy.'

'You cannot say that. He is the best boy in Nazareth. Have you ever heard Him cry, or be naughty, or be disobedient or lack respect?'

'No. That's true. But He will do all that if You continue to spoil Him.'

'You do not necessarily spoil Your children just because you keep them at home. To keep them at home implies loving them with good common sense and wholeheartedly. And that is how we love our Jesus. And since Mary is better educated than a teacher, She will be Jesus' Teacher.'

' And when your Jesus is a Man, He will be like a silly little woman frightened even of flies.'

'He will not. Mary is a strong Woman and She will give Him a manly education. I am not a coward and I can give Him man-like examples. Jesus is a creature without any physical or moral faults. He will, therefore, grow up, upright and strong, both in His body and in His spirit. You can be sure of that, Alphaeus. ....He will not be a disgrace to the family......In any case, that is what I have decided and that is all.'

'Perhaps Mary has decided and you...'

'And if it were so? Is it not fair that two who love each other, should have the same thoughts and the same wishes, so that each may accept the wishes of the other as if they were his own?... If Mary should wish silly things, I would say to Her "No." But She is asking for something that is full of wisdom and I agree, and I make it my own. We love each other, we do as we did the first day, and we shall go on doing so as long as we live. Is that right Mary?'

'Yes, Joseph. And let us hope it will never happen, but when one should die without the other, we will still go on loving each other.'

Joseph gives Mary a pat on the head as though She were a young daughter and She looks at him with Her serene loving eyes.

'You are quite right' Agrees Mary of Alphaeus. 'I wish I could teach! Our children learn both good and evil at school. At home, they only learn what is good. But I do not know whether.....if Mary...'

'What is it you want, My sister-in-law? Speak freely. You know that I love you and I am happy when I can do something that pleases you.'

'I was thinking...James and Judas are only a little older than Jesus. They are already going to school....for what they have learned!...Jesus instead, already knows the law so well....I would like....eh, I mean, if I asked You to take them as well, when You teach Jesus? I think they would behave better and be better educated. After all, they are cousins, and it is only fair that they should love one another like brothers. Oh! I would be so happy!'

'If Joseph wants, and your husband agrees, I am quite

willing. It is the same to speak to one as to speak to three. And it is a joy to go through the whole Bible. Let them come.'

The three children, who have come in quietly, are listening and awaiting the final decision.

'They will drive You to despair, Mary.' says Alphaeus.

'No! They are always good with Me. You will be good if I teach you, will you not?'

The two boys approach and stand on either side of Mary, place their arms around Her shoulders, lean their little heads on Her shoulders and promise all the good in the world.

'Let them try, Alphaeus, and let Me try. I am sure you will not be dissatisfied with the test. They can come every day from the sixth hour (noon) until evening(6pm-Sundown) . It will be enough, believe Me. I know how to teach without tiring them. You must hold their attention and let them relax at the same time. You must understand them, love them and be loved by them, if you wish to get good results. ....And you will love Me, will you not?

And Mary receives two big kisses in answer.

'See?'

' I see. I can only say: "Thank You." And what will Jesus say when He sees His Mummy busy with others? What do You say, Jesus?'

' I say: "Happy are those who listen to Her and build their dwelling near Hers." As for Wisdom, happy are those who are My Mother's friends, and I am happy that those who, I love are Her friends.'

'But who puts such words on the lips of the Child?' asks Alphaeus, astonished.

'Nobody, brother. Nobody in this world.'

And so Mary becomes the Teacher of Jesus, Judas and James and the three boys, cousins, grow to love one another like brothers, growing up together, "like three shoots supported by one pole"......Jesus is Her pupil exactly like His cousins are. And through this semblance of a normal life, the "seal" is kept on God's secret against the investigations of the Evil One.

Preparations for Jesus' Coming of Age

Mary is bending over an earthenware vessel, using a stick to stir at its contents that fill the cool clear air of the kitchen garden with steam.

She is wearing a heavy dark brown dress, so dark, it is almost black, and an apron made of a rough piece of cloth for protection.

Outside, it is the depth of winter and with the exception of the olive trees, all the plants and trees are bare and stand like skeletons against the clear sky, in the beautiful sunshine that does not take the bite off the bitterly cold wind that shakes the bare boughs and the little green-grey branches of the olive trees.

Mary takes out the stick from the vessel, wets Her fingers with the ruby-red drops dripping from it, checks the colour against Her apron and seems satisfied.

She goes into the house and returns with many long loose coils of snow-white wool which She dips carefully and patiently into the vat, one at a time. Whilst She works, Mary of Alphaeus, coming from Joseph's workshop, enters and they greet each other and chat.

'Is it coming alright?' asks Mary of Alphaeus.

'I hope so.'

'That Gentile lady assured me that it is exactly the colour, and that is exactly how they do it in Rome. She gave it to me only because of You, because of the embroidery work you did for Her....She said that not even in Rome is there anyone who can embroider so well. You must have become blind doing it....'

'It was a mere trifle!' says Mary, smiling and shaking Her head.

Mary of Alphaeus looks at the last coils of wool before handing them to Mary. 'How beautifully you have spun them! They are so thin and smooth that they look like hair....You do everything so well. And You are so quick!....will these last ones be of a lighter colour?'

'Yes, they are for the tunic. The mantle is darker.'

Both women work together at the Vat. Then they pull out the coils of a beautiful purple colour, run quickly to dip them in ice-cold water in a little vessel under the thin tumbling spring of softly babbling water, rinsing them over and over again and then laying them on canes fastened to the branches of the trees.

'They will dry well and rapidly in this wind.' says Mary of Alphaeus.

'Let us go to Joseph. There is a fire in there. You must be frozen.' Says Mary. 'It was very kind of you to help Me. I did it very quickly and without working so much. I am very grateful to you.'

'Oh! Mary! What would I not do for You! To be near You is a great joy. And then...all this work is for Jesus. And He is such a dear, Your Son!...I will feel that He is also my Son, if I help You with His feast when He comes of age.'

The two women enter the work shop that smells heavily of planed wood, a typical Carpenter's workshop.

Jesus has grown into a tall, strong, well-built, lean and handsome twelve- year old boy, Who looks older than His years. Already, He reaches His Mothers shoulders and now looks more like a younger brother to His very young Mother. His blond curly hair is now longer, coming down to below His ears and looks like a small golden helmet fully wrought in bright curls, already somewhat darker than when He was a boy, with auburn reflections in it. They are no longer the graceful curls of His childhood and not yet the wavy long hair of His manhood that reached His shoulders, ending in a soft big curl but it already resembles more the latter in its colour and style.

His rosy round face is still the face of a child but later, in His youth and then in His manhood, it will become thinner and lose its rosy colour to become a delicate alabaster with a hue of yellowish pink.

His eyes, still those of a child, are naturally large and wide open, with a sparkle of joy lost in the seriousness of His glance. Later, they will no longer open so wide....His eyelashes will cover half of them to conceal the excessive wickedness He sees in the world from His Pure and Holy Soul. Only when He is working miracles will they be open and bright, brighter than they are now.....to cast out demons, raise the dead, heal diseases and forgive sins. The sparkle of happiness mingled with seriousness also will be lost in the proximity of death, sin and the human knowledge of the uselessness of His sacrifice because of the unwillingness and aversion of man....Only in rare moments of joy, when He is with faithful believers, particularly pure people, mostly children, will His holy, mild, kind eyes shine again with happiness.
Now, he is at home with His Mother and Joseph, smiling lovingly, His little cousins who are admiring Him and His aunt, Mary of Alphaeus, who is patting Him....He is happy....He needs love to be happy and in this moment,

he has love.

He is wearing a beautiful woollen, light ruby-red tunic that hangs down to His ankles so that only His sandal clad feet can be seen. The tunic is loose, perfectly woven in its compact thinness and has long wide sleeves. The hems around the neck, the ends of the sleeves and the bottom which hangs to the ground has a beautiful Greek fret, in a darker shade, woven into the ruby of the garment. It is most beautiful and Mary of Alphaeus admires Mary's work and praises it.

His sandals are new and well made, not simple like the ones He wore as a child

'Here is your Son' says Mary, lifting Jesus' left hand in Her right one. She seems to be introducing Him and confirming His paternity at once. Jesus is smiling. 'Bless Him, Joseph, 'adds Mary ' before leaving for Jerusalem. There was no ritual blessing for His first step in life, because it was not necessary for Him to go to school. But now that He is going to the Temple to be proclaimed of age, please bless Him. And bless Me with Him. Your blessing ...' Mary sobs softly'...will fortify Him and give Me strength to detach Myself a little more from Him...'

'Mary, Jesus will always be Yours. The formality will not affect our mutual relationship. Neither will I content with

You for this Son, so dear to us. No one deserves, as You do, to guide Him in life, O my holy Spouse.'

Bending, Mary takes and kisses Joseph's hand, the respectful loving spouse of Her consort!

Joseph receives the sign of love and respect with dignity then lays the palm of the hand that was kissed on Her head solemnly saying: 'Yes, I bless You, O Blessed One, and I bless Jesus with You....' and he lays the palm of the other hand on Jesus' head '...Come to me, my only joys, my honour and the essence of my life.' pronounces Joseph over the two bowed heads, equally blond and equally holy '... May the Lord look upon You and bless You. May He have mercy on You and give You peace. May the Lord give You His blessing...' and then he adds '...And now, let us go. The hour is favourable for the journey.'

Mary takes a wide dark brown mantle and drapes it over the body of Her Son, tenderly caressing Him as She does so.

They close the door after them and set off for Jerusalem, with other pilgrims going in the same direction.

Outside the village, the women separate from the men but the children are free to go where they like. Jesus stays with

His Mother.

The pilgrims go through the country, beautiful in the spring time, singing psalms most of the time. The meadows and the crops in the fields are fresh and the leaves on the trees have just begun to bloom. In the fields along the road, men sing with them and birds, too, sing their love songs in the branches of the trees. The clear streams reflect, like mirrors, the flowers on their banks and the little lambs jump about staying close to their mothers. There is peace and happiness under the loveliest April sky....

Jesus Examined at the Temple when He is of Age.

It is the feast of the Unleavened Bread (Pasch) and lasts for seven days. The first and the last days of prayer are the most important and so the pilgrims remain in Jerusalem for the duration.

There are People milling in and out of Temple enclosure gates, crossing yards, halls, porches, disappearing in this or that building on the various floors, within the bulk of the Temple.

The group of Jesus' family goes in singing psalms in low voices, the men in front and the women behind. Others have joined them, perhaps from Nazareth or Jerusalem.

The women stop on the lower landing and the men continue to the point from where they worship the Most High.

Then Joseph parts from the rest, and with his Son, goes back through some yards and then goes into a room that looks like a synagogue. He speaks to a Levite, who disappears behind a stripped curtain and returns with some older priests; Doctors of the Law, appointed to examine the believers.

Jesus and Joseph both bow deeply to the ten Doctors, who sit down with dignity on low wooden stools.

'Here.' says Joseph 'This is my Son. Three months and twelve days ago, He reached the age which the law prescribes to become of age. And I want Him to comply with the prescriptions of Israel..... I would ask you to note that His constitution proves that He is no longer in His childhood or minority. ......And I ask you to examine Him kindly and fairly, to judge that what I here, His father, have stated, is the truth. I have prepared Him for this hour and for this dignity of Son of the Law. He knows the precepts, the traditions, the decisions, the customs of the fringes*
and the phylacteries**, He knows how to say the daily prayers and blessings......

* knotted fringes worn on the corners of the prayer shawl to remind the Jews of the commandments of God.
**a small leather box that holds Jewish texts on vellum, worn by Jewish men at morning prayer as a reminder to keep the law

.......therefore, since He knows the law in itself and in its three branches of Halascia, Midrasc and Aggada, He can behave as a man. Therefore, I wish to be free from the responsibilities of His actions and of His sis. From now on, He must be subject to the precepts and He must pay Himself the penalty for His failures towards them. Examine Him.'

'We will. Come forward, Child. What is Your name?'

'Jesus of Joseph, from Nazareth.'

'A Nazarene....Can You therefore read?'

'Yes, rabbi, I can read the words which are written and those which are construed in the words themselves.'

'What do You mean?'

'I mean that I understand also the meaning of the allegory or of the symbol which is hidden under the appearance, as a pearl does not appear but it is inside an ugly closed shell.'

'A clever answer and a very wise one. We seldom hear that on the lips of adults; in a child and a Nazarene in addition!...'

The attention of the ten has been awakened and their eyes do not lose for an instant, the beautiful blond Child, Who is looking at them sure of Himself, with neither boldness nor fear.

'You honour Your master, who certainly, was deeply read.'

'The Wisdom of God was gathered in his just heart.'

'But listen to that! You are a happy man, father of such a Son!'

Joseph, from his place at the end of the room, smiles and bows.

They give Jesus three rolls each tied with a different coloured ribbon.

'Read the one closed with the golden ribbon.'

Jesus opens the roll and reads. It is the Decalogue- the Ten Commandments-, but after a few words, one of the judges takes the roll from Him saying ' Go on by heart.'
Jesus continues, as sure of Himself as though He were reading and every time He mentions the Lord, He bows deeply.

'Who taught You that? Why do You do that?'

'Because the Name is holy and it is to be pronounced with a sign of internal and external respect. Subjects bow to their king, who is king only for a short time and he is dust. To the King of kings, the Most High Lord of Israel, Who is present even if He is only visible to the spirit, shall not every creature bow since every creature depends on Him with eternal subjection?'

'Very clever! Man: we advise you to have your Son educated either by Hillel or Gamaliel. He is a Nazarene...but His answers give us hope that He will become a new great doctor.'

'My Son is of age. He will decide according to His own will. If His decision is an honest one, I will not oppose it.'

'Listen, Child, You said: "Remember to sanctify feast days. Not only for yourself, but also for your son and your daughter, your servant and your maidservant, even for your horse it is said that they must not work on Sabbaths." Now tell me: If a hen lays an egg on a Sabbath or a sheep lambs on a Sabbath, will it be legal to use the fruit of its womb, or will it be considered gross misconduct?'

' I know that many rabbis; Shammai is the last of them and is still alive, say that an egg laid on a Sabbath is against the precept. But I think that there is a difference between man and animals or whoever fulfils a natural act such as giving birth. .....If I compel a horse to work, I am responsible for its sin, because I force it to work with a whip...... But if a hen lays an egg which has matured in its ovary, or a sheep lambs a little one on a Sabbath, because it is ready to be born, no, such a deed is not a sin. ....Neither is the egg laid or the lamb born on a Sabbath a sin in the eyes of God.'

'But why, if every kind of work is a sin on Sabbaths?'

'Because to conceive and give birth corresponds to the will of the Creator and complies with the laws which He gave to every creature.....Now, the hen does nothing but obey the law according to which, after so many hours of growth, an egg is complete and ready to be laid.....And the sheep also obeys the laws laid by Him Who created everything, according to which laws twice a year, when the springtime is on the meadows in bloom, and when the trees in the forest lose their leaves and men muffle themselves up because of the intense cold, sheep should mate so that later they may give milk, meat and nourishing cheese, in the opposite seasons of the year. That is, in the months when the toil for the crops is harder or the bleakness is more painful because of the frostbite. If therefore a sheep, when its time is up, gives birth to a little lamb, oh! Little lamb can also be sacred also on the altar, because it is a fruit of the obedience to the Creator.'

'I would not examine Him any further. His wisdom is greater than that of many grown up people and is really surprising.'

'No. He said that He is capable of understanding also the symbols. Let us hear Him.'

'First, let Him say a psalm, the blessings and the prayers.'

'Also the precepts.'

'Yes, repeat the Midrrasciot.'

Jesus repeats a long litany of "Don't do this.... Don't do that..." without any hesitation.

'That is enough. Open the roll with the green ribbon.'

Jesus opens it and is about to read....

'Further on, yes, further on.'

Jesus obeys.

'That is enough. Now read and explain it, if You think there is a symbol.'

'In the Holy Word, it is seldom missing. It is we who cannot see and apply it. I read: Fourth Book of the Kings, Chapter twenty-two, verse ten: "Then Shaphan, the secretary, informed the king saying: 'Hilkiah, the High Priest, has given me a book'; and Shaphan read it aloud in the king's presence. On hearing the contents of the law of God, the king tore his garments and gave the following.....'

'Read after all the names.'

".... The following order:' Go consult Yahweh, on behalf of me and the people, on behalf of the whole Judah, about the contents of this book that has been found. Great indeed must be the anger of Yahweh blazing out against us because our ancestors did not obey what this book says, by practising everything written in it..."

'That is enough. This happened many centuries ago. Which symbol do You find in an event of ancient history?'

'I find that time cannot be related to what is eternal. And God is eternal. And our soul is eternal. And the relation between God and our soul is also eternal. Therefore the thing that gave rise to a punishment then, is the same thing that gives rise to a punishment now, and the effects of the fault are the same.'

'That is?'

'Israel is no longer acquainted with the Wisdom, which comes from God. It is to Him, and not to poor men, that we must apply for light. And it is not possible to have light if there is no justice and loyalty to God....That is why men sin, and God, in His anger, punishes them.'

'We are no longer acquainted? ....But what are You saying Child? And the six hundred and thirteen precepts?'

'The precepts exist, but there are mere words; we know them but we do not practise them.....that is why we are not acquainted with them. This is the symbol: everyman, in every period of time, must consult the lord to know His will and comply with it to avoid drawing His anger on himself.'

'The Child is perfect. Not even the trap of the tricky question has upset Him in His reply. Let us take Him to the real synagogue.'

They go into a larger, more splendid room where, the first thing they do, is shorten His hair and Joseph picks up His big curls.
Then they tighten His red tunic with a long band wound several times round His waist and tie some little fringes to His forehead, arm and mantle, fixing them on with studs.
Then they sing psalms and Joseph praises the Lord with a long prayer, invoking all blessings on his Son.

The ceremony over, Jesus goes with Joseph to re-join their male relatives, they buy a lamb and offer it as a slaughtered victim before re-joining the women.

Mary kisses Jesus as One She has not seen for many years. She looks at Him, now more manly in His clothes and in the style of His hair, and pats Him....

And then they go out.

Jesus Goes Missing In Jerusalem

After the seven day feast, the holy family together with the other pilgrims who had come from Nazareth, regroup to depart from Jerusalem and return to Nazareth. Once again, as is usual, the men separate from the women, leaving the children free to go with either parent. Jesus takes this opportunity to withdraw from both His parents without their knowledge. Joseph supposes that the Child is with His Mother, as is generally the case, not considering for even one moment that Mary might go without Him, given Her great love for Him.

Mary, for Her part, has fewer reasons for supposing that Jesus might be with Joseph but the Lord Himself so diverts Her thoughts with holy and divine reflections that His absence, at first, goes unnoticed. When eventually, She notices the absence of Her Son by Her side, She then supposes that Jesus has stayed with Joseph for his consolation.

Thus assured, Mary and Joseph journey for a whole day

and the pilgrims thin out as they go their separate ways.
Eventually, Joseph and Mary meet at the appointed place
on the first evening after leaving Jerusalem. It has been a
long day's journey; the beds are made for the pilgrims to
rest. Food is prepared and ready to be handed out. Only
then do they realise that Jesus is with neither parent. They
are struck dumb with amazement and for quite some time,
neither of them can speak. Then Mary starts to tremble,
Her face turns pale, Her eyes open wide but there is no
outburst of tears and cries. Governed by profound humility
as they are, each parent is overwhelmed with self-reproach
for having neglected watching over Jesus, each blaming
themselves for His absence. When they have somewhat
recovered from their astonishment, in deepest sorrow, they
take counsel with each other on what is to be done.

'....My heart cannot rest, unless we return with all haste to
Jerusalem to find my most holy Son.' Says Mary.

They begin their search with family and friends but none
have seen Jesus since the departure from Jerusalem and
their answers only increase Mary and Joseph's anxiety.
They do not stop to eat and though it is dark, they return
to Jerusalem, stopping the caravans and pilgrims on the
way and questioning them. It is another long day's walk
back to Jerusalem and then the feverish search in town
begins.

In tears and groans, they persevere for three whole days, without food or sleep, filled with sorrow and anxiety. During these three days, the Lord leaves Mary to Her natural resources and grace, depriving Her of special privileges, with the exception of the company of the angels. And yet, even in such deep affliction, Mary does not lose Her peace, nor entertain an angry thought, nor allow Herself any improper expression. Neither does She fail in Her reverence and praise of the Lord, nor cease on Her prayers and petitions for the human race.

By God's provision, Mary does not know where to search for many hours. It does not make sense to Her to search for a Child in the Temple where if He had been lost in the town and guided back to the Temple, He might have cried for His Mother and attracted the attention of the people or the Priests who would have helped Him find His Mother with notices left at the gates.

Although Mary's thousand angel guard is witness to Her sorrow, they give Her no clue to help find the Child. Having agreed to split up in order to cover more ground, Joseph and Mary search the streets and alleyways of Jerusalem, describing Him to the women of Jerusalem as 'Beautiful', 'blond', 'Strong' but there are so many like that, it is too little to enable anyone to say for certain that they saw Him here or there.

She decides to go to Bethlehem in the hope that She might find Him in the cave of the Nativity but the angels prevent Her telling Her that He is not so far off.
She finds nothing to indicate that Herod Archelaus- the son of Herod the Great who came to power in 4BC - has taken Jesus prisoner and She begins to firmly believe that He is with John the Baptist.
On the third day, She decides to go find Him where John is but the angels prevent Her telling Her that Her Son is not with John.

Mary can tell from their answers that the angels do know where Her Son is but understand that they withhold the information from Her by the command of the Lord. They continue their search in Jerusalem.

One Woman, confirms that a child fitting that description came to her door the day before to ask for alms, which she gave and she was ravished by the grace and beauty of the child saying;

'When I gave Him alms, I felt myself overcome by compassion to see a Child so gracious in poverty and want'.

This is the first news that Mary gets of Her Beloved in Jerusalem and it gives Her some comfort. She pursues Her quest and meets others who speak of Him in like manner and She follows this trail of information, which takes Her to the city hospital, as She reasons that Jesus would be found amongst the afflicted. At the hospital, She learns that a Child fitting that description did visit, left alms and consoled many. These reports rouse the sweetest most affectionate feelings in Mary's heart and She sends these sweet sentiments forth from the depths of Her heart as messengers to Her lost Son.

Only then does the thought strike Her that if He is not with the poor, then no doubt He would be at the Temple, the house of God and of prayer.

The angels encourage this thought telling Her that the hour of Her consolation is near and urging Her to hasten to the Temple. Joseph, who has been sorrow stricken for the past three days as well, hastening this way and that, sometimes with Mary and other times by himself, without food or rest, is also now ordered to the Temple by another angel and he re-joins Mary.

These three days of anguish for Mary and Joseph is the symbol of three other days of future anguish.

At the end of the three days, Mary, exhausted, enters the Temple, walks along the yards and halls. Nothing. She runs, poor Mother, when She hears the voice of a Child and even the bleatings of the lambs give Her the impression that She hears Her Child weeping and looking for Her. But Jesus is not weeping. He is teaching.

Jesus Disputes with the Doctors in the Temple

It is the third day since Jesus turned back at the City gates having learned the will of the Father. Hastening back through the streets, He knows, by His divine foresight, the suffering this will cause and He offers this suffering to the Father for the benefit of souls. Then for the three days, He asks for alms and takes them to the poor, consoling both those Who give Him alms and those who receive them. He visits the hospital and heals many in body and soul, enlightening them and leading them back to the way of salvation. It is on the third day that He returns to the Temple for a lesson predestined by Providence.

Jesus, in a long white linen tunic reaching to His feet and topped with a pale red rectangular piece of cloth, is leaning against a low wall on a minor road that continues uphill and downhill from where He is. The road is littered with stones and there's a ditch in the middle of it that must turn into a rivulet when it rains. For now, the road is dry because it's a lovely day in the Spring and Jesus is smiling mildly but rather serious, looking around and down over a group of houses in an irregular formation; some tall, others low, and they're all scattered in every direction, like a handful of white stones thrown carelessly on dark soil, with streets and lanes like veins against all that whiteness. Here and there, plants protrude from the walls; some in bloom, others already covered with new leaves.

To His left, is the massive structure of the Temple set on three sets of terraces covered with buildings, towers, yards and porches, in the centre of which is the highest and most magnificent building with its round domes that shine in the sun as though covered with copper and gold. The whole complex is enclosed within a fortified wall with merlons like those of a stronghold. A tower, higher than the others, built over a narrow climbing road, commands a clear view of the huge building-The Temple- and has the air of a heavy- handed sentry.

Jesus stares at the tower then He turns round and leans back against the low wall as He had done before, and now looks at a hillock in front of the building- where the street ends in an arch- its base crowded with houses leaving the rest of it bare.

Beyond the arch, there's a road paved with square stones, which are loose and uneven. As Jesus, looks, His face becomes more serious and clouds with sadness.

There are large crowds gathered in the yards, around the fountains, in the porches and pavilions within the Temple complex, Jews talking loudly and intent on a number of activities.

Pharisees in long flowing dresses, priests in wide white linen tied to their waists with precious belts and with precious plates on the chests and on their foreheads, with other sparkling points here and there on their varied robes. And many others, of the priestly cast, but in less decorative garments, themselves surrounded by younger disciples. These are the doctors of the law.

The doctors stand in groups disputing theology. One of the groups is headed by a doctor called Gamaliel, who is supported by an old man, almost blind, called Hillel, who is perhaps a teacher or relative to Gamaliel judging by the respectful familiarity with which Gamaliel treats the old man. Gamaliel's group is smaller in number and less conservative in their views as opposed to another more numerous group led by a doctor called Shammai, known for his conservative and resentful intolerance.

Surrounded by a compact group of disciples, Gamaliel is talking about the Messiah and founding his observations on Daniel's prophecy, states that the Messiah must already have been born because the seventy weeks prophesied from the time the decree for the reconstruction of the temple was issued, expired some ten years ago.

But Shammai disagrees ad counters that if it were true that the Temple has been rebuilt, then it is also true that Israel has become more enslaved and the peace, which He Whom the prophets called "Prince of Peace" was to bring, is quite far from being in the world, and in Jerusalem in particular. The Town is in fact oppressed by an enemy so bold as to exert his dominion within the Temple walls that are themselves dominated by the Antonia Tower, full of Roman legionaries who are ready to cut down with their swords, any riots that may break out for the independence of the country.

And thus, the dispute drags on endlessly, full of pedantic objections, with all the doctors showing off their learning, not so much to beat their opponents but rather to display themselves for the admiration of the listeners. Their aims are quite obvious.

Then comes the clear voice of a boy from the compact group of believers:

'Gamaliel's right.'

There's a stir in the crowd and in the group of doctors as they look for the interrupter. There is no need to search because He does not hide, but makes His way through the crowd, approaching the group of the rabbis. It is Jesus, sure of Himself and openhearted, eyes sparkling with intelligence.

'Who are You?' they ask Him.

'I am a son of Israel, who has come to fulfil what the law prescribes.'
His bold frank reply gains Him smiles of approval and favour and they take an interest in the young Israelite.

'What is Your name?'

'Jesus of Nazareth.'

The kindness fades away in Shammai's group but Gamaliel, more benign, continues his conversation with Hillel, suggesting that the old man ask the boy something.

'On what do You base Your certainty?' asks Hillel

'On the prophecy, which cannot be wrong about the time and the signs which took place at the time it came true...' answers Jesus '...It is true that Caesar dominates us, but the world and Palestine were in such peace when the seventy weeks expired, that it was possible for Caesar to order a census in his dominions. Had there been wars in the empire and riots in Palestine, he would not have been able to do so.....

...... As that time was completed, so the other time of sixty-two weeks plus one, from the completion of the Temple is also being completed, so that the Messiah may be anointed and the remainder of the prophecy may come true for the people who did not want Him......

.....Can you doubt that? Do you not remember the star that was seen by the Wise Men from the East and stopped over the sky in Bethlehem of Judah, and that the prophecies and visions, from Jacob onwards, indicate that place as the one destined to be the birthplace of the Messiah, son of the son of Jacob's son, through David, who was from Bethlehem?...

......Do you not remember Balaam?...."A star will be born of Jacob." The Wise Men from the East, whose purity and faith opened their eyes and ears, saw the Star and understood its Name: "Messiah", and they came to worship the Light which had descended into the world.'

'Do you mean that the Messiah was born in Bethlehem-

Ephrathah at the time of the Star?' asks Shammai, glaring at Jesus.

'I do.'

'Then he no longer is. Don't you know, Child, that Herod had all the infants born of women from one day old up to the age of two, slaughtered in Bethlehem and surroundings?.....asks Shammai.
.......You, Who are so wise in the Scriptures, must also know this: "A voice is heard in Ramah...it is Rachel weeping for her children." The valleys and the hills in Bethlehem, which gathered the tears of the dying Rachel, were left full of tears, and the mothers have wept again on their slaughtered children. Amongst them, there certainly was the Mother of the Messiah.'

'You are wrong, old man....'says Jesus '....The weeping of Rachel turned into hosannas because there, where she gave birth to "the son of her sorrow", the new Rachel has given the world the Benjamin of the Heavenly Father, the Son of His right hand, Him, Who is destined to gather the people of God under His sceptre and free them from the most dreadful slavery.'

'How can that be if He was killed?' counters Shammai

'Have you not read about Elijah..' asks Jesus '...He was

carried off by the chariot of fire. And could the Lord God not have saved His Immanuel, that He might be the Messiah of His people?......He, Who parted the sea in front of Moses, that Israel might walk on dry ground towards its land, could He not have sent His angels to save His Son, His Christ, from the ferocity of men?.......
......I solemnly tell you:..... ' and Jesus raises and stretches out His right arm in a gesture of command and promise, His voice a sharp sound that fills the air, His eyes brighter than ever '....The Christ is alive and is amongst you....' And when His hour comes, He will show Himself in His power.' And Jesus lowers His arm as one who has sworn an oath. And His solemnity, though He is a boy, is that of a man.

'Child, who taught you these words?' asks Hillel?

'The spirit of God. I have no human teacher. This is the word of the Lord Who speaks to you through my lips.'

'Come near us, that I may see You, Child, and my hope may be revived by Your faith and my soul enlightened by the brightness of Yours.'

They make Jesus sit on a stool between Gamaliel and Hillel and they give Him some rolls to read and explain. It is a proper examination and the people throng and listen.

Jesus reads in a clear voice:" Be consoled, my people. Speak to the heart of Jerusalem and call to her that her time of service is ended.....A voice cries in the wilderness:" Prepare a way for the Lord...then the glory of the Lord shall be revealed..."

'See that, Nazarene...' says Shammai'... It refers here to an ended slavery, but never before have we been slaves as we are now. And there is the mention of the precursor. Where is he? You are talking nonsense.'

'I tell you, that the admonition of the precursor should be addressed to you more than anyone else ...'answers Jesus '...To you and those like you. Otherwise, you will not see the glory of the Lord, neither will you understand the word of God because meanness, pride and falsehood will prevent you from seeing and hearing.'

'How dare You speak to a master like that?' asks Shammai outraged.

'I speak thus. And thus I shall speak even to My death, because above Me, there are the interests of the Lord and the love for the Truth, of which I am the Son....
......And I add, rabbi, that the slavery of which the prophet speaks, and of which I am speaking, is not the one you think, neither is the loyalty the one you consider....
.... On the contrary, by the merits of the Messiah, *man will*

be made free from the slavery of Evil, which separates him from God, and the sign of Christ will be on the spirits, freed from the yoke and made subjects of the eternal kingdom ....

............All the nations will bend their heads, o household of David, before the Shoot born of you and which will grow into a tree that covers the whole world and rises up to Heaven. ....And in Heaven and on the earth every mouth will praise His Name and bend its knee before the Anointed of God, the Prince of Peace, the Leader, before Him, **Who by giving Himself** will fill with joy and nourishment every disheartened and famishing soul, before the Holy One **Who will establish an alliance between Heaven and earth.** .....Not like the Covenant made with the elders of Israel when God led them out of Egypt, treating the, still as servants, *but infusing a heavenly paternity into the souls of men with the Grace instilled once again by the merits of the Redeemer,* through Whom *all good people will know the lord and the Sanctuary of God will no longer be demolished and destroyed.'*

'Do not blaspheme, Child! ....' cries Shammai '...Remember Daniel. He states that after the death of Christ, the temple and the Town will be destroyed by a people and a leader who will come from afar....And You hold that the sanctuary of God will no longer be demolished! ....Respect the Prophets!'

'I solemnly tell you that there is Someone Who is above the Prophets, and you do not know Him and will not know Him because you do not want to.....And I tell you that what I said is true. *The true Sanctuary will not be subject to death. But like its sanctifier it will rise to eternal life and at the end of the world it will live in Heaven.*'

'Listen to me, Child...' says Hillel '... Haggai says: "... The One Expected by the nations will come...great then shall be the glory of this house, and of this last one more than of the previous one." Does he perhaps refer to the Sanctuary of which You speak?'

'Yes, master...' responds Jesus '...That is what he means. Your honesty leads you towards the Light and I tell you: when the sacrifice of Christ is accomplished, you shall have peace because you are an Israelite without wickedness.'

'Tell me, Jesus ...' asks Gamaliel '...How can the peace of which the Prophets speak be hoped for, if destruction is going to come to this people by war? Speak and enlighten me also.'

'Do you not remember, master, what those said, who were present on the night of Christ's birth?' asks Jesus. *That the angels sang: "Peace to men of good will"* but these people are not of goodwill and will not have peace. It will not acknowledge its King, the Just Man, the Saviour, because they expect Him to be a king with human power, *whereas He is the King of the spirit.* They will not love Him, because they will not like what Christ preaches. Christ will not defeat their enemies with their chariots and their horses. *He will instead, defeat the enemies of the soul, who endeavour to imprison in hell, the heart of man which was created for the Lord......*And this is not the victory which Israel is expecting from Him. Your king will come, Jerusalem, riding a "donkey" and a "colt", that is, the just people of Israel and the Gentiles......But I tell you that the colt will be more faithful to Him and will follow Him preceding the donkey and will grow in the ways of Truth and life. *Because of its evil will, Israel will lose its peace and suffer for centuries and will cause its King to suffer and will make Him the King of sorrow of Whom Isaiah speaks.'*

'Your mouth tastes of milk and blasphemy at the same time, Nazarene...'accuses Shammai '...Tell me: where is the precursor? When did we have him?'

'He is' answers Jesus. ' Does not Malachi say: Here I am going to send My messenger to prepare the way before Me; and the Lord you are seeking will suddenly enter His Temple, and the angel of the Covenant Whom you are longing for?" .... *Therefore, the Precursor immediately precedes Christ. He already is, as Christ is. If years should elapse between him who prepares the ways for the Lord and Christ, all the ways will become obstructed and twisted again.* God knows and arranges beforehand that the Precursor should precede the Master by *one hour only*.....When you see this Precursor, you will be able to say: "The mission of Christ is beginning." And I say to you: Christ will open many eyes and many ears when He comes this way. But He will not open yours or those of people like you, because you will be putting to death, Him Who is bringing you life......But when the Redeemer sits on His throne and on His altar, Higher up than this Temple....Higher than the Tabernacle enclosed in the Holy of Holies,.....higher up than the Glory supported by the Cherubim, ...Maledictions for the deicides and life for the Gentiles will flow from His thousands and thousands of wounds, because He, o master, who are unaware of it, is not, I repeat, is not the king of a human kingdom, *but a spiritual Kingdom ....and His subjects will be only those who for His sake will learn to regenerate in the spirit* and like Jonah, after being born, *will learn to be born again, on other shores: "The shores of God"* by means of a spiritual regeneration which will take place through Christ, Who will give humanity true life.'

'This Nazarene is Satan!' cry Shammai and his followers.

'No. This Child is a Prophet of God!' cry Hillel and his followers

'Stay with me, Child. My old age will transfuse what I know into Your knowledge and You will be Master of the people of God.'

'I solemnly tell you that if there were many like you, salvation would come to Israel. But My hour has not come. *Voices from Heaven speak to Me and in solitude I must gather them until My hour comes.* Then with My lips and My blood I will speak to Jerusalem, and the destiny of Prophets stoned and killed by her, will also be My destiny......
......But above my life there is the Lord God, to Whom I submit Myself as a faithful servant, to make of Myself a stool for His glory.....waiting that He will make the world a stool at the feet of Christ..... *Wait for Me in My hour. These stones shall hear My voice again and vibrate hearing My last word......*'

And then, Mary, Who is still searching the Temple grounds for Her Beloved hears His voice, all of a sudden, from beyond the barrier of a large group of people. She hears Him saying "....*These stones shall hear My voice again and vibrate hearing My last word.....*" She tries to make Her way through the crowds......meanwhile Jesus is still speaking ....

'.......Blessed are those who in that voice would have heard God and believed in Him because of it. To them, Christ will give that kingdom which your selfishness imagines to be a human one, whereas it is a heavenly one ....'

And Jesus stands up in the midst of the astonished doctors and with His arms outstretched and His face raised to Heaven, burning with spiritual ardour, he continues...

'........and therefore I say: *"Here is Your servant Lord, Who has come to do Your will. Let it be consummated, because I am eager to fulfil it.*'

After much effort, Mary succeeds to make Her way through the large crowds. And there is Her Son, standing, arms outstretched in the midst of the doctors of the law. Prudent Virgin that She always is, this time, Her anxiety is like a hurricane that overcomes even Her prudence and She runs to Her Son, embraces Him, lifting Him off the stool and putting Him down on the ground.

'Oh! Why have You done this to us!' She exclaims 'For three days we have been looking for You. Your Mummy is dying with pain. Your father is exhausted with fatigue. Why, Jesus?'

But you do not ask "why" of Him Who knows. "Why" He behaves in a certain way. Why those with a vocation leave everything and follow the voice of God. Jesus is Wisdom and He knows; fulfilling the mission He is called to, putting the interests of the Divine Father above those of His earthly father and mother.

And Jesus tells Mary so, finishing His teaching of the doctors with a lesson to the Queen of doctors.

Mary takes that lesson and keeps it in Her heart. His words deeply rooted in Her mind.

And the sun begins to shine in Her heart again now that She has Her Jesus, humble and obedient, beside Her. There will be much sunshine and many clouds; great joys and many tears alternating in Her heart during the next twenty one years. But never again, will She ask "why."

www.ingramcontent.com/pod-product-compliance
Lightning Source LLC
Chambersburg PA
CBHW061333040426
42444CB00011B/2903